INCREDIBLE INSECTS

BEES

James E. Gerholdt

Published by Abdo & Daughters, 4940 Viking Drive, Suite 622, Edina, Minnesota 55435.

Printed in the United States.

Cover Photo credit: Peter Arnold, Inc.
Interior Photo credits: Peter Arnold, Inc.

Edited by Julie Berg

Library of Congress Cataloging-in-Publication Data

Gerholdt, James E., 1943
    Bees / by James E. Gerholdt.
    p. cm. — (Incredible insects)
    Glossary and index.
    ISBN 1-56239-483-5
1. Bees—Juvenile literature. [1. Bees.] I. Title. II . Series:
Gerholdt, James E., 1943- Incredible insects.
QL565.2.G47   1995
595.79'9—dc20   95-5444
                                                   CIP
                                                    AC

Contents

BEES

Bees belong to one of the 28 insect orders. Ants and wasps also belong to the same order. Insects are arthropods. This means their skeleton is on the outside of their body. They also are ectothermic—they get their body heat from the environment. There are at least 280,000 species in this order, 22,000 of which are bees. They are found worldwide.

Bees have four transparent wings, a mouth that can chew, and long antennae. Some bees, such as honeybees and bumblebees, are social insects. This means they help each other care for and defend the hive, or nest. They also help gather food and care for the young. But most bees are solitary, which means they live alone, not in a large group.

Right:
Most bees live alone,
not in a large group.

LIFE CYCLE

All bees go through a complete metamorphosis. This means there are four stages in their life cycle. Most bees hatch from eggs that are laid underground or in any hole the female can find. Honeybees lay their eggs in cells inside the hive.

After the eggs hatch, the young spend the first part of their life as larvae. In the social species, adult bees feed the larvae which then enter the pupa stage. The honeybee's role in the hive depends on the food they ate as larvae. Most bees are workers, some are drones, and a few are queens.

**Right:
Honeybee larvae
inside the beehive.**

SIZES

Bees are not very large. The honeybee's body is only 7/16 of an inch (11 mm) long and fat. Other bees, like the cuckoo bees, are smaller. Their body is only 3/8 of an inch (9.5 mm) long and not as fat. The wingspan is usually about twice as wide as the body is long.

Bumblebees can grow to almost 1 inch (2.5 cm) but their wings are not as long as other bees. The queens of the social bees, such as bumblebees and honeybees, are often twice the size of the workers and drones.

**Right:
The honeybee's
wingspan is usually
about twice as wide as
the body is long.**

SHAPES

Wing shape is one way to identify different bee species. A bee's body is usually covered with many hairs. These hairs collect pollen when a bee lands on a flower. The pollen is then combed off onto the hind legs, and into the pollen basket. Some bees don't have a pollen basket. They carry the pollen under the body.

Like all insects, bees have three body parts: the head, thorax, and abdomen. They also have six legs and a pair of antennae.

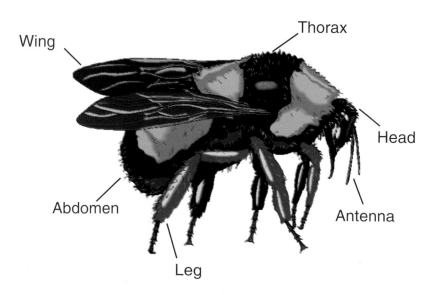

Wing

Thorax

Head

Abdomen

Antenna

Leg

Right: The hairs on a honeybee collect pollen when it lands on a flower.

10

COLORS

Most bees are yellow with black markings, but some are black with yellow markings. Sometimes a bumblebee has orange instead of yellow markings.

Several bee species have different colors. Halictid bees may be brown or a bright metallic green. Andrenid bees are dark brown or black. Both groups are found in the United States. All bees' wings are transparent.

**Right:
This bumblebee has
orange, yellow, and
black markings.**

WHERE THEY LIVE

Bees live in many different habitats, such as deserts, woods, fields, and gardens. But wherever they are, bees need flowers! Many species rely on one plant type for their food.

Besides flowers, bees also need nesting places. Favorite sites are holes in the ground and wood, snail shells, hollow twigs, and cracks in old walls. Honeybees use box-like hives that humans make for them. Here the queen lays her eggs which have been fertilized by the drones.

**Right:
Bees building their
honeycomb-shaped
hive.**

SENSES

Bees have the same five senses as humans. Their keen eyesight helps them find flowers.

Social bees, like the honeybees, actually have a language! When a good pollen source is found, the bee returns to the hive and alerts the others. The bee will use a dance to tell them where to go. Movements and buzzing tell the others how much pollen there is and how far away it is. The other bees use their antennae and hearing to understand the dance.

Right:
The compound
eyes of a bee.

DEFENSE

A bee's best defense is to fly away from an enemy. It can also sting! But only the workers have stingers. When a bee stings, the stinging barb injects a venom. Then the whole stinging barb and venom gland pull away, eventually killing the bee. Not all species can sting. Some, like the stingless bees, use their mouth to bite an enemy.

Defending the hive is the most important task of any social bee. If a predator attacks the hive, an alarm is given off that the other bees smell. Then the bees hurry to help defend the hive. While a single sting usually is not dangerous, many stings are!

**Right:
Bees work very hard
to defend their hives.
This is an African
killer bee hive.**

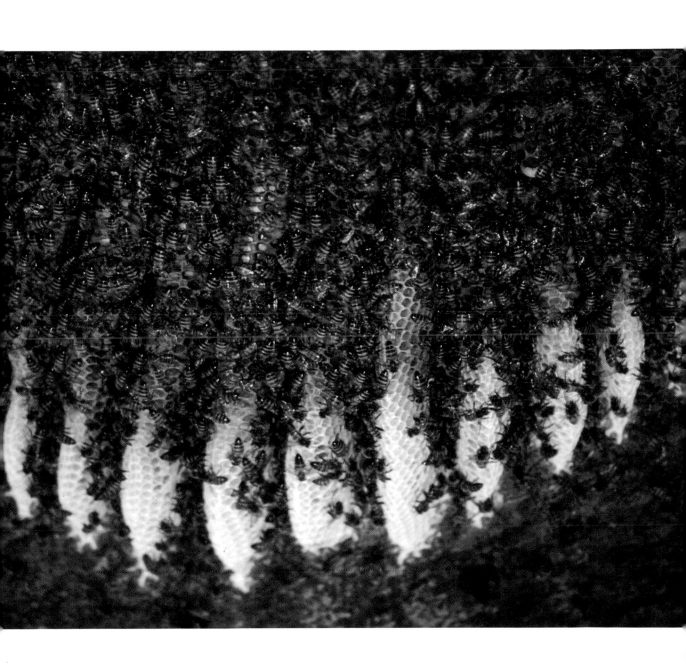

FOOD

Bees feed on pollen. The pollen is collected on the hind legs or under the body and carried back to the hive or the spot where the eggs have been laid. Honeybees make a royal jelly, or bee milk, to feed the larvae. This is all the future queens eat. The larvae are only fed for a few days. After that they eat honey and pollen.

Bees are very valuable to humans. Without them, flowers and crops such as clover, cotton, and apples would not be pollinated and grow. We are glad that bees are part of our world.

Without bees, there would be no honey! A bee collects nectar, which is stored in the body in a honey sac. The bee then deposits it into the cells of the hive, where it is also used as food in the winter.

Right:
Bees feed on
flower pollen.

GLOSSARY

Abdomen (AB-doe-men) - The rear body part of an arthropod.

Antennae (an-TEN-eye) - A pair of sense organs found on the head of an insect.

Arthropod (ARTH-row-pod) - An animal with its skeleton on the outside of its body.

Drone - A male bee, without a stinger.

Ectothermic (ek-toe-THERM-ik) - Regulating body temperature from an outside source.

Environment (en-VI-ron-ment) - Surroundings in which an animal lives.

Habitat (HAB-uh-tat) - An area in which an animal lives.

Insect - An arthropod with three body parts and six legs.

Larva - The second stage of an insect that goes through a complete metamorphosis.

Metamorphosis (met-a-MORF-oh-sis) - The change from an egg to an adult.

Nectar - A sweet liquid formed in many flowers, used by bee's in the making of honey.

Pollen - The powdery substance produced by flowers that contain the male cells.

Pollinate (POLL-i-nate) - To carry pollen to another plant.

Predator (PREAD-a-tore) - An animal that eats other animals.

Pupa (PEW-pa) - The third stage of an insect that goes through a complete metamorphosis.

Queen - The female bee in the hive that lays eggs.

Saliva (suh-LIE-vuh) - The liquid made by mouth glands that keep it moist, help in chewing, and start digestion.

Social - Living with others, rather than alone.

Solitary (SOL-ih-tair-e) - Living alone.

Species (SPEE-seas) - A kind or type.

Venom (VENN-um) - A poisonous fluid.

Worker - The female bees in the hive that do all of the work.

INDEX

About the Author

Jim Gerholdt has been studying reptiles and amphibians for more than 40 years. He has presented lectures and displays throughout the state of Minnesota for nine years. He is a founding member of the Minnesota Herpetological Society and is active in conservation issues involving reptiles and amphibians in India, Aruba, and Minnesota.

Photo by Tim Judy